Mojo for AI Engineers

Accelerating Large Language Model Workflows

Dennis Mullis

Table of contents

Introduction

Chapter 1: Mojo Fundamentals for LLM Optimization

Chapter 2: Data Preprocessing and Pipeline Optimization

- 2.1 Efficient Data Loading and Manipulation with Mojo.
- 2.2 Text Preprocessing for LLMs: Tokenization and Encoding.
- 2.3 Building High-Performance Data Pipelines.

Chapter 3: Accelerating LLM Inference

- 3.1 Optimizing Inference Speed: Techniques and Best Practices.
- 3.2 Implementing Custom Inference Kernels.
- 3.3 Batching and Parallelization for Enhanced Throughput.

Chapter 4: Custom Kernel Development for LLM Operations

- 4.1 Designing Custom Kernels for Key LLM Operations.
- 4.2 Low-Level Optimization for Maximum Performance.
- 4.3 Benchmarking and Performance Analysis.

Chapter 5: Deployment and Scaling LLM Applications

- 5.1 Strategies for Deploying Mojo-Powered LLM Applications.
- 5.2 Scaling LLM Applications for Production Environments.
- 5.3 Cloud and Edge Deployment Considerations.

Chapter 6: Advanced Mojo Techniques and Best Practices

- 6.1 Advanced Mojo Features for Complex LLM Projects.
- 6.2 Debugging and Profiling Mojo Code.
- 6.3 Best Practices for Large-Scale LLM Development.

Chapter 7: The Future of LLMs and Mojo

- 7.1 Emerging Trends in LLM Technology.
- 7.2 The Evolving Mojo Ecosystem and Community.
- 7.3 Potential Future Applications of Mojo in AI.

Introduction

Welcome, fellow AI engineers! You're holding this book because, like me, you're passionate about pushing the boundaries of Large Language Models (LLMs). But let's be honest, we've all hit that wall: the sheer computational cost of these models can be… well, a bit of a nightmare. We're talking about massive datasets, complex calculations, and the constant struggle to squeeze every ounce of performance out of our hardware.

Why Mojo for LLM Development? Addressing the Performance Gap.

That's where Mojo comes in. Think of it as a supercharged Python. We all love Python's ease of use and rich ecosystem, right? But when it comes to raw performance, especially for demanding tasks like LLM inference or training, it can leave us wanting. We end up juggling multiple languages – Python for prototyping, C++ or CUDA for performance-critical sections – a frustrating dance we call the "two-language problem."

Mojo aims to solve this. Imagine a language that's as easy to write as Python but performs like C++. That's the promise of Mojo. It gives us the best of both worlds: the development speed we're used to, and the raw power we need for our LLM workloads.

Personally, I've spent countless hours optimizing Python code for LLMs, and trust me, it can feel like trying to build a race car with duct tape. Mojo feels like finally getting the right tools for the job. It allows us to write performant code without sacrificing readability or developer productivity.

Here's why Mojo is a game-changer for LLM developers:

- **Performance:** Mojo is designed to be significantly faster than Python, often rivaling or exceeding the performance of C++. This is crucial for handling the massive computational demands of LLMs.
- **Python Interoperability:** You can seamlessly integrate Mojo with your existing Python code. This means you don't have to rewrite everything from scratch. You can gradually migrate your codebase, optimizing performance-critical parts with Mojo.
- **Hardware Acceleration:** Mojo gives you direct access to hardware features like SIMD and

vectorization, allowing you to fine-tune your code for maximum performance.

- **Memory Management:** Mojo provides fine-grained control over memory allocation and deallocation, which is essential for handling large datasets and models.

In essence, Mojo empowers us to build faster, more efficient LLM applications without sacrificing the ease of development.

Setting Up Your Mojo Environment: Essential Tools and Configuration.

Alright, let's get our hands dirty and set up our Mojo environment. Don't worry, it's a straightforward process.

First, you'll need to install the Modular SDK, which includes the Mojo compiler and runtime. Head over to the Modular.com website and follow their installation instructions. They keep their installation instructions very up to date, so it is the best place to get the most recent information.

- **Installing the Modular SDK:** The official Modular documentation will guide you through the process, which typically involves downloading and running an installer.

- **Setting up your IDE:** while you can use any text editor, Modular also provides good plugin support for VS code, and other editors. This will give you syntax highlighting, and other helpful tools.
- **Verifying the installation:** Once installed, open your terminal and type `mojo --version`. If everything is set up correctly, you should see the Mojo version number.

Now, let's write our first Mojo program. Open your favorite text editor and create a file named `hello.mojo`. Type the following code:

Code snippet

```
fn main():
    print("Hello, Mojo!")
```

Save the file and run it from your terminal using the following command:

Bash

```
mojo hello.mojo
```

You should see "Hello, Mojo!" printed on your screen. Congratulations, you've just run your first Mojo program!

In this book, we'll dive deeper into Mojo's features and explore how to use them to accelerate your LLM workflows. We'll cover everything from data preprocessing and model optimization to deploying and scaling your applications.

So, buckle up, and let's embark on this exciting journey together. I'm excited to see what we can build with Mojo.

Chapter 1: Mojo Fundamentals for LLM Optimization

So we've got our environment set up, and we're ready to dive into the heart of Mojo. This chapter is all about laying the groundwork, getting comfortable with the language, and understanding the core concepts that make Mojo a powerhouse for LLM development. Let's get started!

1.1 Mojo Syntax and Core Concepts: A Swift Introduction

If you're coming from Python, you'll find a lot that's familiar, but also some key differences that unlock incredible performance. Think of Mojo as Python's turbocharged sibling. Let's get started.

Functions: The Building Blocks

Like Python, Mojo revolves around functions. But Mojo introduces static typing, which makes a world of difference.

Code snippet

```
fn add(x: Int, y: Int) -> Int:

    return x + y


fn main():

    let result = add(5, 10)

    print(result) # Output: 15
```

Notice the fn keyword, which is how we define functions. And those type annotations (x: Int, y: Int, -> Int)? They tell the compiler exactly what types of data our function expects and returns. This might seem like extra work, but it catches errors early and allows for significant performance gains.

Variables: let **and** var

Mojo has two keywords for variables: let for immutable variables (think of them as constants) and var for mutable variables.

Code snippet

```
fn main():

    let immutable_value: Int = 10

    var mutable_value: Int = 20


    mutable_value = 30 # Valid

    # immutable_value = 40 # Error!
```

Immutability helps prevent accidental modifications and improves code reliability. `let` is your friend when you want to ensure a value stays constant.

Structs: Custom Data Types

Mojo's `struct` is a powerful tool for defining custom data types. It's similar to Python's classes, but with a focus on performance.

Code snippet

```
struct Point:

    x: Float32
```

```
    y: Float32


fn main():

    let p = Point{x: 1.0, y: 2.0}

    print(p.x, p.y)
```

Structs allow you to group related data together, and they're highly efficient in memory. They are extremely valuable for representing complex data structures that are common in LLM development.

Static Typing: The Performance Edge

Static typing is a core concept in Mojo. It means that the compiler knows the type of every variable and expression at compile time. This allows for:

- **Early Error Detection:** Type errors are caught before runtime, preventing unexpected crashes.
- **Optimized Code Generation:** The compiler can generate highly efficient machine code because it knows the exact data types.

- **Improved Performance:** Static typing eliminates the overhead of dynamic type checking.

Personal Insight:

When I first encountered static typing in Mojo, it felt a bit restrictive compared to Python's dynamic nature. But I quickly realized the performance benefits. The compiler can make assumptions and optimizations that simply aren't possible in a dynamically typed language. And when you're dealing with the massive datasets and complex computations of LLMs, every bit of performance counts.

Key Concepts to Remember:

- `fn`: Used to define functions.
- `let` **and** `var`: Used to declare immutable and mutable variables, respectively.
- `struct`: Used to define custom data types.
- **Static Typing:** A core feature that enables performance optimizations.

Mojo's syntax is designed to be familiar to Python developers, but its static typing and low-level features unlock a new level of performance. By understanding these core concepts, you'll be well on your way to building high-performance LLM applications.

1.2 Memory Management in Mojo: Efficiency and Control

Memory management: it's the unsung hero of high-performance computing. In Python, we often take it for granted, relying on the garbage collector to handle the dirty work.But for LLMs, where memory usage can skyrocket, we need more control. Mojo gives us that control.

Manual Memory Management: The Power and the Responsibility

Unlike Python's automatic garbage collection, Mojo allows for manual memory allocation and deallocation. This means we can directly manage memory using functions like `malloc` and `free`.

Code snippet

```
from memory import malloc, free


fn main():

    let size = 10 * size_of[Float32]()

    let ptr = malloc[Float32](size)


    # Use the memory...


    free(ptr)
```

Why would we want to do this? Well, manual memory management gives us:

- **Predictability:** We know exactly when memory is allocated and deallocated, eliminating unpredictable pauses from garbage collection.
- **Efficiency:** We can optimize memory usage for specific workloads, reducing memory footprint and improving performance.

- **Control:** We have fine-grained control over memory allocation, allowing us to implement custom memory management strategies.

Structs and Memory Layout

Mojo's `struct` plays a crucial role in memory management. Structs allow us to define custom data types with specific memory layouts.

Code snippet

```
struct MyData:

    data: Array[Float32]

    size: Int


fn main():

    let my_data = MyData{data: [1.0, 2.0, 3.0], size: 3}

    # ...
```

By carefully designing our structs, we can minimize memory fragmentation and improve cache locality.

Memory Alignment

Memory alignment is another important aspect of memory management. Modern CPUs can access aligned memory more efficiently. Mojo allows us to control memory alignment, ensuring that our data is accessed optimally.

Personal Insight:

When I first started working with manual memory management, it felt a bit daunting. I was used to the safety net of Python's garbage collector. But I quickly realized the performance gains. By carefully managing memory, I was able to reduce memory usage and improve the speed of my LLM applications. It does come with the responsibility of making sure you free the memory you allocate, or you will get a memory leak. I found that it greatly helped to design the memory allocation and deallocation patterns early in the development process.

Key Concepts to Remember:

- `malloc` **and** `free`: Functions for manual memory allocation and deallocation.
- **Structs:** Custom data types with specific memory layouts.
- **Memory Alignment:** Ensuring data is aligned for optimal access.

Mojo's memory management features give us the tools to build high-performance LLM applications.By understanding and mastering these concepts, we can unlock the full potential of our hardware.

1.3 Harnessing Hardware Acceleration: SIMD and Vectorization

We've explored the basics of Mojo, and now it's time to unleash the true power of our hardware. LLMs thrive on parallel computations, and Mojo gives us direct access to SIMD (Single Instruction, Multiple Data) and vectorization. Let's see how we can leverage these features.

Understanding SIMD and Vectorization

Imagine performing the same operation on multiple data elements simultaneously. That's the essence of SIMD. Modern CPUs have dedicated SIMD instructions that allow us to process vectors of data in parallel.

Mojo provides built-in support for SIMD, making it easy to write vectorized code. This can lead to significant performance gains, especially for operations like matrix multiplication and element-wise arithmetic, which are common in LLMs.

Practical Implementation: Vector Addition

Let's start with a simple example: vector addition. We'll use Mojo's SIMDVector type to represent vectors.

Code snippet

```
from simd import SIMDVector

from math import Float32


fn vector_add(a: SIMDVector[Float32, 4], b:
SIMDVector[Float32, 4]) -> SIMDVector[Float32, 4]:

    """
```

Performs element-wise addition of two SIMD vectors.

Args:

a: The first SIMD vector.

b: The second SIMD vector.

Returns:

The result of the element-wise addition.

"""

return a + b

fn main():

"""

Demonstrates vector addition using SIMD.

"""

```
let a: SIMDVector[Float32, 4] = SIMDVector[Float32,
4](1.0, 2.0, 3.0, 4.0)

let b: SIMDVector[Float32, 4] = SIMDVector[Float32,
4](5.0, 6.0, 7.0, 8.0)

let result = vector_add(a, b)

print(result) # Output: SIMDVector[Float32, 4](6.0, 8.0,
10.0, 12.0)
```

Step-by-Step Explanation:

1. **Import Modules:** We import the `SIMDVector` type from the `simd` module and `Float32` from the `math` module.

2. **Define `vector_add` Function:** This function takes two `SIMDVector[Float32, 4]` arguments and returns their element-wise sum.

3. **Create SIMD Vectors:** We create two `SIMDVector` instances, `a` and `b`, with four `Float32` elements each.

4. **Perform Addition:** We call the `vector_add` function to add the vectors.

5. **Print Result:** We print the result, which is another `SIMDVector`.

Practical Implementation: Matrix Multiplication with SIMD

Now, let's tackle a more complex example: matrix multiplication. We'll use SIMD to accelerate the inner loop of the multiplication.

Code snippet

```
from simd import SIMDVector

from math import Float32

from algorithm import range


fn matrix_multiply_simd(a: Array[Array[Float32]], b: Array[Array[Float32]], c: Array[Array[Float32]]):

    """

    Performs matrix multiplication using SIMD.
```

Args:

    a: The first matrix.

    b: The second matrix.

    c: The result matrix.

"""

```
let rows_a = a.size()

let cols_a = a[0].size()

let cols_b = b[0].size()


for i in range(rows_a):

    for j in range(cols_b):

        var sum_vector: SIMDVector[Float32, 4] =
SIMDVector[Float32, 4](0.0, 0.0, 0.0, 0.0)

        for k in range(0, cols_a, 4):

            let a_vector: SIMDVector[Float32, 4] =
SIMDVector[Float32, 4](
```

```
                a[i][k], a[i][k + 1], a[i][k + 2], a[i][k + 3]

        )

        let b_vector: SIMDVector[Float32, 4] =
SIMDVector[Float32, 4](

            b[k][j], b[k + 1][j], b[k + 2][j], b[k + 3][j]

        )

        sum_vector += a_vector * b_vector

    c[i][j] = sum_vector[0] + sum_vector[1] +
sum_vector[2] + sum_vector[3]


fn main():
    """

    Demonstrates matrix multiplication using SIMD.

    """

    let a: Array[Array[Float32]] = [[1.0, 2.0, 3.0, 4.0], [5.0,
6.0, 7.0, 8.0]]
```

```
let b: Array[Array[Float32]] = [[9.0, 10.0], [11.0, 12.0],
[13.0, 14.0], [15.0, 16.0]]

let c: Array[Array[Float32]] = [[0.0, 0.0], [0.0, 0.0]]



matrix_multiply_simd(a, b, c)

print(c)
```

Step-by-Step Explanation:

1. **Import Modules:** We import the necessary modules.
2. **Define** `matrix_multiply_simd` **Function:** This function performs matrix multiplication using SIMD.
3. **Iterate Through Matrices:** We iterate through the rows and columns of the matrices.
4. **Create SIMD Vectors:** We create `SIMDVector` instances from the elements of the matrices.
5. **Perform Vector Multiplication and Addition:** We use SIMD instructions to perform the multiplication and addition.
6. **Store Result:** We store the result in the `c` matrix.

Personal Insight:

When I first started experimenting with SIMD, I was amazed by the performance gains. Vectorizing my code allowed me to significantly speed up my LLM applications. But it requires careful attention to data alignment and memory access patterns.

Key Concepts to Remember:

- **SIMD:** Single Instruction, Multiple Data.
- **Vectorization:** Performing operations on vectors of data.
- `SIMDVector`: Mojo's type for representing SIMD vectors.

1.4 Python Interoperability: Seamless Integration Strategies

One of Mojo's most compelling features is its ability to seamlessly integrate with Python. We don't have to throw away our existing Python code and libraries. Instead, we can gradually migrate to Mojo, optimizing performance-critical sections while leveraging the vast Python ecosystem.Let's see how.

Understanding Python Interoperability

Mojo's Python interoperability allows us to import Python modules directly into our Mojo code and call Python functions. This is incredibly useful for:

- **Leveraging Existing Libraries:** We can use popular Python libraries like NumPy, Pandas, and Hugging Face Transformers.
- **Gradual Migration:** We can migrate our code to Mojo incrementally, optimizing performance-critical parts first.
- **Prototyping:** We can use Python for rapid prototyping and then convert performance-sensitive sections to Mojo.

Practical Implementation: Importing and Using NumPy

Let's start with a simple example: importing and using NumPy.

Code snippet

from python import Python

fn main():

    """

    Demonstrates importing and using NumPy in Mojo.

    """

    let np = Python.import_module("numpy")

    let arr = np.array([1, 2, 3, 4, 5])

    print(arr)

    let squared_arr = np.square(arr)

    print(squared_arr)

Step-by-Step Explanation:

1. **Import** `Python` **Module:** We import the `Python` module, which provides the interface for Python interoperability.
2. **Import NumPy Module:** We use `Python.import_module("numpy")` to import the NumPy module.
3. **Create NumPy Array:** We call `np.array()` to create a NumPy array.
4. **Print Array:** We print the NumPy array.
5. **Use NumPy Function:** We call `np.square()` to square the elements of the array.
6. **Print Squared Array:** We print the squared array.

Practical Implementation: Calling Python Functions with Arguments

We can also call Python functions with arguments and retrieve their return values.

Code snippet

from python import Python

```
fn main():

    """

    Demonstrates calling a Python function with
    arguments in Mojo.

    """

    let math = Python.import_module("math")

    let result = math.pow(2.0, 3.0)

    print(result)
```

Step-by-Step Explanation:

1. **Import** `Python` **Module:** We import the `Python` module.
2. **Import Math Module:** We import the math module.
3. **Call Python Function:** We call the `math.pow()` function with arguments `2.0` and `3.0`.
4. **Print Result:** We print the return value of the function.

Practical Implementation: Interacting with Python Objects

Mojo can interact with python objects.

Code snippet

```
from python import Python
```

```
fn main():

    let my_list = Python.list([1,2,3,4,5])

    my_list.append(6)

    print(my_list)
```

Step-by-Step Explanation:

1. **Import** `Python` **Module:** We import the `Python` module.
2. **Create Python List:** We create a python list.
3. **Use Python List Methods:** We append to the python list.
4. **Print Result:** We print the altered python list.

Personal Insight:

When I started using Mojo, the ability to integrate with Python was a huge relief. It allowed me to leverage my existing Python knowledge and libraries while gradually migrating to Mojo. This made the transition much smoother and more efficient. I found that I would keep the data loading and high level model architecture in python, and then move the most computationally expensive model layers into mojo.

Key Concepts to Remember:

- `Python.import_module()`: Imports a Python module.
- **Calling Python Functions:** We can call Python functions directly from Mojo.
- **Python Object interactions:** We can interact with python objects from within Mojo.

Chapter 2: Data Preprocessing and Pipeline Optimization

We've got our Mojo fundamentals down. Now, let's tackle a crucial part of any LLM workflow: data preprocessing. You know, the stuff that makes or breaks your model's performance. In this chapter, we'll explore how to leverage Mojo's speed and efficiency to build lightning-fast data pipelines.

2.1 Efficient Data Loading and Manipulation with Mojo

Data is the lifeblood of LLMs. But handling massive datasets efficiently is no easy feat. Mojo gives us the tools to load and manipulate data with speed and precision.Let's dive in.

Understanding Efficient Data Loading

The key to efficient data loading is minimizing I/O operations and memory overhead. Mojo's low-level control allows us to optimize these aspects.

- **Streaming Data:** Instead of loading the entire dataset into memory, we can stream data in chunks.
- **Binary Data Formats:** Using binary data formats (like `.bin` or `.npy`) can reduce file size and improve loading speed.
- **Memory Mapping:** Memory mapping allows us to treat files as memory, eliminating the need for explicit read/write operations.

Practical Implementation: Reading a Text File Line by Line

Let's start with a basic example: reading a text file line by line.

Code snippet

```
from io import File


fn process_lines(filepath: String):

    """

    Reads a text file line by line and processes each line.
```

```
    Args:

        filepath: The path to the text file.

    """

    let file = File(filepath, "r")

    if file.is_valid():

        for line in file.lines():

            # Process each line here

            print(line)

        file.close()


fn main():

    """

    Demonstrates reading a text file line by line.

    """

    process_lines("data.txt")
```

Step-by-Step Explanation:

1. **Import `File` Module:** We import the `File` module from the `io` library.
2. **Define `process_lines` Function:** This function takes a file path as input and reads the file line by line.
3. **Open File:** We open the file using `File(filepath, "r")`.
4. **Iterate Through Lines:** We use a `for` loop to iterate through the lines of the file.
5. **Process Line:** We process each line (in this case, we simply print it).
6. **Close File:** We close the file using `file.close()`.

Practical Implementation: Reading Binary Data

For numerical data, binary formats are much more efficient.

Code snippet

from io import File

```
from memory import DTypePointer

from math import Float32


fn read_binary_data(filepath: String) -> Array[Float32]:

    """

    Reads binary data from a file and returns an array of
Float32.


    Args:

        filepath: The path to the binary file.

    """

    let file = File(filepath, "rb")

    if file.is_valid():

        let file_size = file.size()

        let num_floats = file_size / size_of[Float32]()

        let data = Array[Float32].alloc(num_floats)
```

```
    let ptr: DTypePointer[Float32] = data.data()

    file.read(ptr.to_byte_pointer(), file_size)

    file.close()

    return data

else:

    return []



fn main():

    """

    Demonstrates reading binary data from a file.

    """

    let data = read_binary_data("data.bin")

    print(data)
```

Step-by-Step Explanation:

1. **Import Modules:** We import the necessary modules.
2. **Define** `read_binary_data` **Function:** This function reads binary data from a file.
3. **Open File:** We open the file in binary read mode (`"rb"`).
4. **Calculate Size:** We calculate the number of `Float32` values in the file.
5. **Allocate Array:** We allocate an array to store the data.
6. **Read Data:** We use `file.read()` to read the binary data into the array.
7. **Close File:** We close the file.
8. **Return Array:** We return the array of `Float32` values.

Practical Implementation: Manipulating Data with Structs

Mojo's `struct` allows us to define custom data structures for efficient data manipulation.

Code snippet

```
struct DataRecord:

    id: Int

    value: Float32


fn process_records(records: Array[DataRecord]):

    """

    Processes an array of DataRecord structs.


    Args:

        records: The array of DataRecord structs.

    """

    for record in records:

        print(record.id, record.value * 2.0)


fn main():

    """
```

Demonstrates manipulating data with structs.

"""

```
let records = [DataRecord{id: 1, value: 10.0},
DataRecord{id: 2, value: 20.0}]

process_records(records)
```

Personal Insight:

When I started working with large datasets, I quickly realized the importance of efficient data loading and manipulation. Mojo's low-level control allowed me to optimize these operations, resulting in significant performance gains. I found the ability to define custom data structures with structs to be extremely valuable for organizing and processing complex data.

Key Concepts to Remember:

- **Streaming Data:** Processing data in chunks.
- **Binary Data Formats:** Using binary formats for numerical data.
- **Structs:** Defining custom data structures for efficient manipulation.

By mastering these techniques, you can build high-performance data pipelines for your LLM applications.

2.2 Text Preprocessing for LLMs: Tokenization and Encoding

LLMs don't understand raw text directly. They need numbers! So, we need to transform our text data into numerical representations. This process involves two key steps: tokenization and encoding. Let's get started!

Understanding Tokenization and Encoding

- **Tokenization:** Breaking down text into smaller units (tokens). These can be words, subwords, or characters.
- **Encoding:** Mapping these tokens to numerical IDs.

Efficient tokenization and encoding are crucial for LLM performance. Mojo allows us to create custom routines that are significantly faster than Python-based solutions.

Practical Implementation: Basic Word Tokenization

Let's start with a simple word tokenizer that splits text by spaces.

Code snippet

```
fn tokenize_words(text: String) -> Array[String]:

    """

    Tokenizes a string into words by splitting on spaces.


    Args:

        text: The input string.


    Returns:

        An array of tokens.

    """

    var tokens: Array[String] = []

    var current_token: String = ""

    for char in text:
```

```
    if char == ' ':

        if current_token != "":

            tokens.push(current_token)

            current_token = ""

        else:

        current_token += char

    if current_token != "":

        tokens.push(current_token)

    return tokens


fn main():

    """

    Demonstrates basic word tokenization.

    """

    let text = "This is a sample text for tokenization"

    let tokens = tokenize_words(text)
```

```
print(tokens)
```

Step-by-Step Explanation:

1. **Define** `tokenize_words` **Function:** This function takes a string as input and returns an array of tokens.
2. **Iterate Through Characters:** We iterate through the characters of the input string.
3. **Build Tokens:** We build tokens by accumulating characters until we encounter a space.
4. **Append Tokens:** We append completed tokens to the `tokens` array.
5. **Return Tokens:** We return the array of tokens.

Practical Implementation: Encoding Tokens with a Vocabulary

Now, let's encode these tokens using a vocabulary (a mapping from tokens to IDs).

Code snippet

from collections import Map

```
fn encode_tokens(tokens: Array[String], vocabulary:
Map[String, Int]) -> Array[Int]:

    """

    Encodes tokens using a vocabulary.


    Args:

        tokens: The array of tokens.

        vocabulary: The vocabulary (token to ID mapping).


    Returns:

        An array of encoded tokens.

    """

    var encoded_tokens: Array[Int] = []

    for token in tokens:

        if token in vocabulary:

            encoded_tokens.push(vocabulary[token])
```

```
        else:

            encoded_tokens.push(0) # Unknown token

    return encoded_tokens


fn main():

    """

    Demonstrates encoding tokens with a vocabulary.

    """

    let text = "This is a sample text for tokenization"

    let tokens = tokenize_words(text)

    let vocabulary: Map[String, Int] = {"this": 1, "is": 2, "a":
3, "sample": 4, "text": 5, "for": 6, "tokenization": 7}

    let encoded_tokens = encode_tokens(tokens,
vocabulary)

    print(encoded_tokens)
```

Step-by-Step Explanation:

1. **Import** `Map` **Module:** We import the `Map` module for creating the vocabulary.
2. **Define** `encode_tokens` **Function:** This function takes an array of tokens and a vocabulary as input and returns an array of encoded tokens.
3. **Iterate Through Tokens:** We iterate through the tokens.
4. **Lookup Token ID:** We look up the token's ID in the vocabulary.
5. **Append Token ID:** We append the token's ID to the `encoded_tokens` array.
6. **Handle Unknown Tokens:** We use a default ID (0) for unknown tokens.
7. **Return Encoded Tokens:** We return the array of encoded tokens.

Personal Insight:

When I first started working with LLMs, I underestimated the importance of efficient tokenization and encoding. I was using Python libraries, and the performance was terrible. Switching to Mojo allowed me to write custom routines that were significantly faster. Also, I found that using sub-word tokenization, like byte pair encoding, greatly improved the performance of my models, and Mojo allows for very high performance implementations of that.

Key Concepts to Remember:

- **Tokenization:** Breaking down text into tokens.
- **Encoding:** Mapping tokens to numerical IDs.
- **Vocabulary:** The token-to-ID mapping.
- **Sub-word tokenization:** More advanced tokenization that splits words into sub-word units.

2.3 Building High-Performance Data Pipelines

We've covered data loading, manipulation, tokenization, and encoding. Now, let's stitch it all together into a high-performance data pipeline. A pipeline is a series of steps that transform raw data into the format our LLM expects. Mojo lets us build these pipelines with incredible efficiency.

Understanding Data Pipelines

A data pipeline typically involves the following stages:

1. **Data Ingestion:** Loading raw data from various sources.

2. **Data Transformation:** Cleaning, filtering, and preprocessing the data.
3. **Tokenization and Encoding:** Converting text data into numerical representations.
4. **Batching and Shuffling:** Organizing data into batches for efficient model training.
5. **Data Output:** Delivering the processed data to the LLM.

Practical Implementation: A Simple Text Data Pipeline

Let's build a simple pipeline that reads text data from a file, tokenizes and encodes it, and creates batches.

Code snippet

```
from io import File

from collections import Map


struct DataRecord:

    encoded_tokens: Array[Int]
```

```
    label: Int


fn tokenize_words(text: String) -> Array[String]:

    # (Same tokenization function as in 2.2)

    var tokens: Array[String] = []

    var current_token: String = ""

    for char in text:

        if char == ' ':

            if current_token != "":

                tokens.push(current_token)

                current_token = ""

        else:

            current_token += char

    if current_token != "":

        tokens.push(current_token)

    return tokens
```

```
fn encode_tokens(tokens: Array[String], vocabulary:
Map[String, Int]) -> Array[Int]:

    # (Same encoding function as in 2.2)

    var encoded_tokens: Array[Int] = []

    for token in tokens:

        if token in vocabulary:

            encoded_tokens.push(vocabulary[token])

        else:

            encoded_tokens.push(0) # Unknown token

    return encoded_tokens



fn process_data(filepath: String, vocabulary: Map[String,
Int]) -> Array[DataRecord]:

    """

    Processes text data from a file and returns an array of
DataRecord structs.
```

Args:

    filepath: The path to the text file.

    vocabulary: The vocabulary (token to ID mapping).

Returns:

    An array of DataRecord structs.

"""

```
var data_records: Array[DataRecord] = []

let file = File(filepath, "r")

if file.is_valid():

    for line in file.lines():

        let parts = line.split(",")

        if parts.size() == 2:

            let text = parts[0]

            let label = parts[1].to_int()
```

```
        let tokens = tokenize_words(text)

        let encoded_tokens = encode_tokens(tokens,
vocabulary)

        let record = DataRecord{encoded_tokens:
encoded_tokens, label: label}

        data_records.push(record)

    file.close()

    return data_records


fn main():
    """"""

    Demonstrates a simple text data pipeline.

    """"""

    let vocabulary: Map[String, Int] = {"this": 1, "is": 2, "a":
3, "sample": 4, "text": 5, "for": 6, "tokenization": 7}

    let data = process_data("data.csv", vocabulary)

    print(data)
```

Step-by-Step Explanation:

1. **Define** `DataRecord` **Struct:** We define a struct to represent a data record.

2. **Define** `tokenize_words` **and** `encode_tokens` **Functions:** (Same as in 2.2).

3. **Define** `process_data` **Function:** This function reads data from a CSV file, tokenizes and encodes the text, and creates `DataRecord` structs.

4. **Open File:** We open the CSV file.

5. **Iterate Through Lines:** We iterate through the lines of the file.

6. **Split Line:** We split each line into text and label.

7. **Tokenize and Encode Text:** We tokenize and encode the text.

8. **Create DataRecord:** We create a `DataRecord` struct.

9. **Append DataRecord:** We append the `DataRecord` to the `data_records` array.

10. **Return Data Records:** We return the array of `DataRecord` structs.

11. **Main Function:** We create a vocabulary and call `process_data` to process the data.

Practical Implementation: Batching and Shuffling

For efficient model training, we need to batch and shuffle our data.

Code snippet

from random import shuffle

fn create_batches(data: Array[DataRecord], batch_size: Int) -> Array[Array[DataRecord]]:

    """

    Creates batches from an array of DataRecord structs.

    Args:

        data: The array of DataRecord structs.

        batch_size: The batch size.

    Returns:

An array of batches.
"""

```
var batches: Array[Array[DataRecord]] = []

var current_batch: Array[DataRecord] = []

for record in data:

    current_batch.push(record)

    if current_batch.size() == batch_size:

        batches.push(current_batch)

        current_batch = []

if current_batch.size() > 0:

    batches.push(current_batch)

return batches


fn main():

    # ... (process_data from previous example) ...

    let batches = create_batches(data, 2)
```

```
shuffle(batches) # Shuffle Batches

print(batches)
```

Personal Insight:

When I started building complex LLM pipelines, I realized the importance of modularity and efficiency. Mojo allowed me to create highly optimized pipelines that significantly improved training speed. Also, I found that using memory mapped files, when dealing with very large datasets, was a massive performance boost.

Key Concepts to Remember:

- **Data Pipeline:** A series of steps that transform raw data.
- **Batching:** Grouping data into batches for efficient training.
- **Shuffling:** Randomizing the order of data to prevent bias.
- **Modularity:** Breaking down the pipeline into reusable components.

Chapter 3: Accelerating LLM Inference

We've prepped our data, and now it's time to put our LLMs to work. But let's be real – LLM inference can be slow. Like, "grab a coffee and watch a movie" slowly. In this chapter, we'll explore how to use Mojo to supercharge our inference pipelines and get those models running at lightning speed.

3.1 Optimizing Inference Speed: Techniques and Best Practices

We've built our data pipelines, and now it's time to make our LLMs run fast. Real fast. Inference speed is crucial for many applications, especially those requiring real-time responses. Mojo gives us the tools to achieve lightning-fast inference.

Understanding Inference Optimization

Inference optimization involves a combination of algorithmic improvements and low-level code tuning. We aim to reduce latency and increase throughput.

- **Algorithmic Optimizations:** Choosing efficient algorithms and data structures.
- **Code Optimizations:** Minimizing memory allocations, leveraging SIMD, and optimizing loops.
- **Hardware Optimizations:** Taking advantage of specific hardware features (e.g., CPU caches, GPU acceleration).

Practical Implementation: Minimizing Memory Allocations

Memory allocation is an expensive operation. We can significantly improve inference speed by reusing memory buffers.

Code snippet

```
from math import Float32

from algorithm import range


fn matrix_multiply(a: Array[Array[Float32]], b:
Array[Array[Float32]], c: Array[Array[Float32]]):
```

```
"""
Performs matrix multiplication with memory reuse.

Args:
    a: The first matrix.
    b: The second matrix.
    c: The result matrix (pre-allocated).
"""

let rows_a = a.size()

let cols_a = a[0].size()

let cols_b = b[0].size()


for i in range(rows_a):

    for j in range(cols_b):

        var sum: Float32 = 0.0

        for k in range(cols_a):
```

```
            sum += a[i][k] * b[k][j]

        c[i][j] = sum


fn main():

    """

    Demonstrates matrix multiplication with memory
reuse.

    """

    let a: Array[Array[Float32]] = [[1.0, 2.0], [3.0, 4.0]]

    let b: Array[Array[Float32]] = [[5.0, 6.0], [7.0, 8.0]]

    let c: Array[Array[Float32]] = [[0.0, 0.0], [0.0, 0.0]] #
pre-allocated


    matrix_multiply(a, b, c)

    print(c)
```

Step-by-Step Explanation:

1. **Pre-allocate Result Matrix:** We pre-allocate the c matrix, so we don't need to allocate memory in the inner loop.
2. **Perform Matrix Multiplication:** We perform the matrix multiplication as usual.
3. **Store Result:** We store the result in the pre-allocated c matrix.

Practical Implementation: Leveraging SIMD for Vector Operations

We can use SIMD to perform vector operations in parallel, significantly speeding up computations.

Code snippet

from simd import SIMDVector

from math import Float32

from algorithm import range

fn vector_add(a: SIMDVector[Float32, 4], b: SIMDVector[Float32, 4]) -> SIMDVector[Float32, 4]:

```
    """

    Performs element-wise addition of two SIMD vectors.


    Args:

        a: The first SIMD vector.

        b: The second SIMD vector.


    Returns:

        The result of the element-wise addition.

    """

    return a + b


fn main():

    """

    Demonstrates vector addition using SIMD.

    """
```

```
let a: SIMDVector[Float32, 4] = SIMDVector[Float32,
4](1.0, 2.0, 3.0, 4.0)

let b: SIMDVector[Float32, 4] = SIMDVector[Float32,
4](5.0, 6.0, 7.0, 8.0)

let result = vector_add(a, b)

print(result)
```

Step-by-Step Explanation:

1. **Import** `SIMDVector` **Module:** We import the
   `SIMDVector` type.
2. **Define** `vector_add` **Function:** This function
   performs element-wise addition of two SIMD
   vectors.
3. **Create SIMD Vectors:** We create two
   `SIMDVector` instances.
4. **Perform Vector Addition:** We use the + operator
   to perform the vector addition.
5. **Print Result:** We print the result.

Practical Implementation: Loop Unrolling

Loop unrolling reduces loop overhead by processing multiple elements per iteration.

Code snippet

from math import Float32

from algorithm import range

fn array_sum_unrolled(arr: Array[Float32]) -> Float32:

"""

Calculates the sum of an array using loop unrolling.

Args:

arr: The input array.

Returns:

The sum of the array.

```
    """

    let size = arr.size()

    var sum: Float32 = 0.0

    for i in range(0, size, 4):

        if i + 3 < size:

            sum += arr[i] + arr[i + 1] + arr[i + 2] + arr[i + 3]

        else:

            for j in range(i, size):

                sum += arr[j]

    return sum


fn main():

    """

    Demonstrates loop unrolling.

    """
```

```
let arr: Array[Float32] = [1.0, 2.0, 3.0, 4.0, 5.0, 6.0, 7.0,
8.0, 9.0, 10.0]

let result = array_sum_unrolled(arr)

print(result)
```

Personal Insight:

When I started optimizing inference speed, I was
surprised by the impact of seemingly small changes.
Memory reuse, vectorization, and loop unrolling can
make a huge difference. I also found that using profiling
tools to identify bottlenecks was essential.

Key Concepts to Remember:

- **Memory Reuse:** Minimizing memory allocations.
- **SIMD:** Performing vector operations in parallel.
- **Loop Unrolling:** Reducing loop overhead.
- **Profiling:** Identifying performance bottlenecks.

3.2 Implementing Custom Inference Kernels

We've explored general optimization techniques. Now,
let's dive into the core of high-performance inference:
custom kernels. These are low-level functions tailored to

specific hardware and LLM operations, allowing us to squeeze out every last bit of performance.

Understanding Custom Kernels

Custom kernels are essentially highly optimized functions written for specific hardware architectures. They're particularly useful for:

- **Performance-Critical Operations:** Matrix multiplications, attention mechanisms, activation functions.
- **Hardware-Specific Optimizations:** Leveraging SIMD instructions, optimizing cache usage.
- **Fine-Grained Control:** Bypassing high-level abstractions for maximum efficiency.

Practical Implementation: Custom Matrix Multiplication Kernel

Let's build a custom kernel for matrix multiplication, a fundamental operation in LLMs.

Code snippet

```
from math import Float32

from algorithm import range


fn matrix_multiply_kernel(a: Array[Array[Float32]], b: Array[Array[Float32]], c: Array[Array[Float32]]):
    """

    Custom kernel for matrix multiplication.


    Args:

        a: The first matrix.

        b: The second matrix.

        c: The result matrix.
    """

    let rows_a = a.size()

    let cols_a = a[0].size()
```

```
    let cols_b = b[0].size()


    for i in range(rows_a):

        for j in range(cols_b):

            var sum: Float32 = 0.0

            for k in range(cols_a):

                sum += a[i][k] * b[k][j]

            c[i][j] = sum


fn main():
    """

    Demonstrates the custom matrix multiplication kernel.

    """

    let a: Array[Array[Float32]] = [[1.0, 2.0], [3.0, 4.0]]

    let b: Array[Array[Float32]] = [[5.0, 6.0], [7.0, 8.0]]

    let c: Array[Array[Float32]] = [[0.0, 0.0], [0.0, 0.0]]
```

```
matrix_multiply_kernel(a, b, c)

print(c)
```

Step-by-Step Explanation:

1. **Define** `matrix_multiply_kernel` **Function:**
   This function performs matrix multiplication.
2. **Iterate Through Matrices:** We iterate through the rows and columns of the matrices.
3. **Perform Multiplication and Addition:** We perform the element-wise multiplication and addition.
4. **Store Result:** We store the result in the `c` matrix.

Practical Implementation: Optimized Activation Function Kernel

Activation functions are another critical part of LLMs. Let's build an optimized kernel for the ReLU activation function.

Code snippet

from math import Float32

```
from algorithm import range


fn relu_kernel(input: Array[Float32], output:
Array[Float32]):

    """

    Custom kernel for the ReLU activation function.


    Args:

        input: The input array.

        output: The output array.

    """

    let size = input.size()

    for i in range(size):

        if input[i] > 0.0:

            output[i] = input[i]

        else:
```

```
        output[i] = 0.0


fn main():

    """

    Demonstrates the custom ReLU kernel.

    """

    let input: Array[Float32] = [-1.0, 2.0, -3.0, 4.0]

    let output: Array[Float32] = [0.0, 0.0, 0.0, 0.0]


    relu_kernel(input, output)

    print(output)
```

Step-by-Step Explanation:

1. **Define** `relu_kernel` **Function:** This function performs the ReLU activation.
2. **Iterate Through Input Array:** We iterate through the elements of the input array.

3. **Apply ReLU:** We apply the ReLU function (output = max(0, input)).
4. **Store Result:** We store the result in the `output` array.

Personal Insight:

When I started writing custom kernels, I felt like I was unlocking a new level of performance. I was able to achieve significant speedups by tailoring my code to the specific hardware and LLM operations. However, writing custom kernels can be challenging. It requires a deep understanding of the hardware and the algorithms.

Key Concepts to Remember:

- **Custom Kernels:** Low-level functions optimized for specific hardware and LLM operations.
- **Hardware-Specific Optimizations:** Leveraging SIMD, cache optimization, etc.
- **Fine-Grained Control:** Bypassing high-level abstractions for maximum efficiency.

3.3 Batching and Parallelization for Enhanced Throughput

We've optimized individual inference operations with custom kernels. Now, let's scale up our inference pipeline to handle multiple requests simultaneously. This is where batching and parallelization come into play, significantly boosting our throughput.

Understanding Batching and Parallelization

- **Batching:** Grouping multiple inference requests into a single batch and processing them together. This reduces overhead and improves efficiency.
- **Parallelization:** Distributing the workload across multiple CPU cores or even GPUs to execute computations concurrently.

These techniques are essential for handling high-volume inference demands.

Practical Implementation: Batching Inference Requests

Let's start by implementing batching. We'll simulate inference requests and process them in batches.

Code snippet

```
struct InferenceRequest:

    input_data: Array[Float32]

    request_id: Int


fn run_inference(input_data: Array[Float32]) ->
Array[Float32]:

    """

    Simulates an inference operation.


    Args:

        input_data: The input data for inference.


    Returns:
```

The output of the inference.

"""

Replace with actual inference logic

var output_data: Array[Float32] = []

for value in input_data:

    output_data.push(value * 2.0)

return output_data

fn process_batch(batch: Array[InferenceRequest]) -> Array[(Int, Array[Float32])]:

"""

Processes a batch of inference requests.

Args:

    batch: The batch of inference requests.

```
    Returns:

        An array of (request_id, output_data) tuples.

    """

    var results: Array[(Int, Array[Float32])] = []

    for request in batch:

        let output_data = run_inference(request.input_data)

        results.push((request.request_id, output_data))

    return results


fn main():

    """

    Demonstrates batching inference requests.

    """

    let requests: Array[InferenceRequest] = [

        InferenceRequest{input_data: [1.0, 2.0, 3.0],
request_id: 1},
```

InferenceRequest{input_data: [4.0, 5.0, 6.0], request_id: 2},

InferenceRequest{input_data: [7.0, 8.0, 9.0], request_id: 3},

InferenceRequest{input_data: [10.0, 11.0, 12.0], request_id: 4},

```
]


let batch_size = 2

var batches: Array[Array[InferenceRequest]] = []

var current_batch: Array[InferenceRequest] = []


for request in requests:

    current_batch.push(request)

    if current_batch.size() == batch_size:

        batches.push(current_batch)

        current_batch = []
```

```
if current_batch.size() > 0:

    batches.push(current_batch)


for batch in batches:

    let results = process_batch(batch)

    print(results)

}
```

Step-by-Step Explanation:

1. **Define** `InferenceRequest` **Struct:** We define a struct to represent an inference request.
2. **Define** `run_inference` **Function:** This function simulates an inference operation.
3. **Define** `process_batch` **Function:** This function processes a batch of inference requests.
4. **Create Inference Requests:** We create an array of `InferenceRequest` structs.
5. **Create Batches:** We group the requests into batches of size `batch_size`.

6. **Process Batches:** We call `process_batch` to process each batch.
7. **Print Results:** We print the results.

Practical Implementation: Basic Parallelization with Threads (Conceptual)

Mojo's parallelization capabilities are evolving. Here's a conceptual example to illustrate how we might parallelize inference using threads.

- **Note:** Mojo's threading model is subject to change. Consult the latest Mojo documentation for accurate and up-to-date implementation.

Code snippet

```
# Conceptual Example (subject to change)

# from threading import Thread



# fn process_request_parallel(request:
InferenceRequest) -> (Int, Array[Float32]):

#    let output_data = run_inference(request.input_data)
```

```
#    return (request.request_id, output_data)


# fn process_batch_parallel(batch:
Array[InferenceRequest]) -> Array[(Int, Array[Float32])]:

#    var results: Array[(Int, Array[Float32])] = []

#    var threads: Array[Thread] = []


#    for request in batch:

#        let thread = Thread(target:
process_request_parallel, args: [request])

#        threads.push(thread)

#        thread.start()


#    for thread in threads:

#        thread.join()

#        results.push(thread.result())
```

return results

Personal Insight:

When I started working with high-throughput inference, I quickly realized that batching and parallelization were essential. They allowed me to handle significantly more requests per second. However, parallelization can be complex, and it's crucial to avoid race conditions and other concurrency issues. Always check the latest Mojo documentation for the most correct method of implementing multi threading.

Key Concepts to Remember:

- **Batching:** Grouping requests for efficient processing.
- **Parallelization:** Executing computations concurrently.
- **Threads:** Lightweight units of execution.

Chapter 4: Custom Kernel Development for LLM Operations

We're moving into advanced territory! We're going to roll up our sleeves and build custom kernels – the heart of high-performance LLM operations. If you want to squeeze every last drop of performance out of your hardware, this chapter is for you.

4.1 Designing Custom Kernels for Key LLM Operations

We've covered general optimization techniques. Now, let's get into the heart of high-performance LLM inference: designing custom kernels. Kernels are the low-level functions that directly interact with the hardware, allowing us to maximize performance for critical LLM operations.

Understanding Kernel Design

Kernel design involves tailoring functions to specific hardware architectures and LLM operations. We aim to:

- **Exploit Hardware Features:** Leverage SIMD instructions, optimize memory access patterns, and utilize specialized hardware units.
- **Optimize Critical Operations:** Focus on matrix multiplications, attention mechanisms, activation functions, and other performance-sensitive operations.
- **Minimize Overhead:** Bypass high-level abstractions and reduce function call overhead.

Practical Implementation: Custom Kernel for Matrix Multiplication

Matrix multiplication is a cornerstone of LLMs. Let's design a custom kernel for it.

Code snippet

from math import Float32

from algorithm import range

```
fn matrix_multiply_kernel(a: Array[Array[Float32]], b:
Array[Array[Float32]], c: Array[Array[Float32]]):

    """

    Custom kernel for matrix multiplication.


    Args:

        a: The first matrix.

        b: The second matrix.

        c: The result matrix.

    """

    let rows_a = a.size()

    let cols_a = a[0].size()

    let cols_b = b[0].size()


    for i in range(rows_a):

        for j in range(cols_b):
```

```
        var sum: Float32 = 0.0

        for k in range(cols_a):

            sum += a[i][k] * b[k][j]

        c[i][j] = sum


fn main():
    """

    Demonstrates the custom matrix multiplication kernel.

    """

    let a: Array[Array[Float32]] = [[1.0, 2.0], [3.0, 4.0]]

    let b: Array[Array[Float32]] = [[5.0, 6.0], [7.0, 8.0]]

    let c: Array[Array[Float32]] = [[0.0, 0.0], [0.0, 0.0]]


    matrix_multiply_kernel(a, b, c)

    print(c)

}
```

Step-by-Step Explanation:

1. **Define** `matrix_multiply_kernel` **Function:** This function performs matrix multiplication.
2. **Iterate Through Matrices:** We iterate through the rows and columns of the matrices.
3. **Perform Multiplication and Addition:** We perform the element-wise multiplication and addition.
4. **Store Result:** We store the result in the `c` matrix.

Practical Implementation: Custom Kernel for Attention Mechanisms

Attention mechanisms are crucial in transformer models. Let's design a custom kernel for the softmax part of the attention.

Code snippet

```
from math import exp, Float32

from algorithm import range


fn softmax_kernel(input: Array[Float32], output: Array[Float32]):
```

```
"""
Custom kernel for the softmax function.

Args:
    input: The input array.
    output: The output array.
"""
let size = input.size()
var max_val: Float32 = input[0]
for i in range(1, size):
    if input[i] > max_val:
        max_val = input[i]

var sum_exp: Float32 = 0.0
for i in range(size):
    output[i] = exp(input[i] - max_val)
```

```
        sum_exp += output[i]


    for i in range(size):

        output[i] /= sum_exp


fn main():
    """

    Demonstrates the custom softmax kernel.

    """

    let input: Array[Float32] = [1.0, 2.0, 3.0, 4.0]

    let output: Array[Float32] = [0.0, 0.0, 0.0, 0.0]


    softmax_kernel(input, output)

    print(output)

}
```

Step-by-Step Explanation:

1. **Define** `softmax_kernel` **Function:** This function performs the softmax operation.
2. **Find Maximum Value:** We find the maximum value in the input array.
3. **Calculate Exponentials:** We calculate the exponentials of the input values.
4. **Calculate Sum of Exponentials:** We calculate the sum of the exponentials.
5. **Normalize Exponentials:** We normalize the exponentials by dividing them by the sum.
6. **Store Result:** We store the result in the `output` array.

Personal Insight:

When I started designing custom kernels, I realized the importance of understanding the underlying hardware. Knowing how the CPU cache and SIMD instructions work allowed me to write much more efficient code. Also, profiling becomes extremely important when writing kernels.

Key Concepts to Remember:

- **Hardware Awareness:** Tailoring kernels to specific hardware architectures.
- **Operation Optimization:** Focusing on performance-critical LLM operations.
- **Low-Level Control:** Minimizing overhead and maximizing efficiency.

4.2 Low-Level Optimization for Maximum Performance

We've designed custom kernels to optimize specific LLM operations. Now, let's delve into the realm of low-level optimization. This is where we fine-tune our code to squeeze out every last bit of performance from the hardware.

Understanding Low-Level Optimization

Low-level optimization involves:

- **Memory Management:** Controlling memory allocation and access patterns.
- **Instruction-Level Parallelism:** Exploiting CPU features like SIMD and pipelining.

- **Cache Optimization:** Minimizing cache misses for faster data access.
- **Hardware Intrinsics:** Using specialized CPU instructions for specific tasks.

Practical Implementation: Memory Alignment

Modern CPUs can access aligned memory much more efficiently. Let's see how we can align memory in Mojo.

Code snippet

```
from memory import malloc, free, align_up

from math import Float32


fn aligned_malloc(size: Int, alignment: Int) ->
DTypePointer[Float32]:

    """

    Allocates aligned memory.


    Args:
```

size: The number of elements to allocate.

alignment: The desired memory alignment.

Returns:

A pointer to the allocated memory.

"""

```
let ptr = malloc[Float32](size * size_of[Float32]())

let aligned_ptr = align_up(ptr.to_byte_pointer(),
alignment).to_dtype_pointer[Float32]()

return aligned_ptr
```

```
fn main():
    """

    Demonstrates aligned memory allocation.

    """

    let size = 10
```

```
let alignment = 32 # 32-byte alignment

let aligned_ptr = aligned_malloc(size, alignment)


# Use the aligned memory...


free(aligned_ptr)

}
```

Step-by-Step Explanation:

1. **Import Modules:** We import the necessary modules.
2. **Define `aligned_malloc` Function:** This function allocates aligned memory.
3. **Allocate Memory:** We allocate memory using `malloc`.
4. **Align Memory:** We use `align_up` to align the memory address.
5. **Return Aligned Pointer:** We return the aligned pointer.

6. **Main Function:** We demonstrate how to use `aligned_malloc`.

7. **Free Memory:** We free the allocated memory using `free`.

Practical Implementation: SIMD Intrinsics (Conceptual)

Mojo's SIMD capabilities are evolving. Here's a conceptual example to illustrate how we might use SIMD intrinsics.

- **Note:** Mojo's SIMD intrinsics are subject to change. Consult the latest Mojo documentation for accurate and up-to-date implementation.

Code snippet

```
# Conceptual Example (subject to change)

# from simd import SIMDVector

# from math import Float32
```

```
# fn vector_multiply_add(a: SIMDVector[Float32, 4], b:
SIMDVector[Float32, 4], c: SIMDVector[Float32, 4]) ->
SIMDVector[Float32, 4]:

#     """

#     Performs a fused multiply-add operation using SIMD
intrinsics.

#     """

#     return a * b + c


# fn main():

#     let a: SIMDVector[Float32, 4] = SIMDVector[Float32,
4](1.0, 2.0, 3.0, 4.0)

#     let b: SIMDVector[Float32, 4] = SIMDVector[Float32,
4](5.0, 6.0, 7.0, 8.0)

#     let c: SIMDVector[Float32, 4] = SIMDVector[Float32,
4](9.0, 10.0, 11.0, 12.0)

#     let result = vector_multiply_add(a, b, c)

#     print(result)
```

```

Personal Insight:

When I started diving into low-level optimization, I was amazed by the performance gains. But it's a complex and challenging process. It requires a deep understanding of the hardware and the compiler. I found that profiling was essential to identify bottlenecks and validate my optimizations. Also, remember that low level optimisations can reduce code readability, so document your code well.

Key Concepts to Remember:

* **Memory Alignment:** Ensuring data is aligned for optimal access.

* **SIMD Intrinsics:** Using specialized CPU instructions.

* **Cache Optimization:** Minimizing cache misses.

* **Profiling:** Identifying performance bottlenecks.

4.3 Benchmarking and Performance Analysis

We've designed custom kernels and applied low-level optimizations. But how do we know if our efforts are paying off? That's where benchmarking and performance analysis come in. They allow us to measure the impact of our optimizations and identify remaining bottlenecks.

Understanding Benchmarking and Performance Analysis

- **Benchmarking:** Measuring the performance of our code under controlled conditions.
- **Profiling:** Identifying performance bottlenecks and hot spots in our code.
- **Performance Analysis:** Interpreting the results of benchmarking and profiling to understand the impact of our optimizations.

Practical Implementation: Simple Benchmarking with Time Measurement

Let's start with a simple benchmark that measures the execution time of a function.

Code snippet

```
from time import now

from math import Float32

from algorithm import range


fn matrix_multiply_kernel(a: Array[Array[Float32]], b:
Array[Array[Float32]], c: Array[Array[Float32]]):

    """

    Custom kernel for matrix multiplication.

    """

    let rows_a = a.size()

    let cols_a = a[0].size()

    let cols_b = b[0].size()


    for i in range(rows_a):

        for j in range(cols_b):

            var sum: Float32 = 0.0
```

```
        for k in range(cols_a):

            sum += a[i][k] * b[k][j]

        c[i][j] = sum


fn benchmark_matrix_multiply():

    """

    Benchmarks the matrix_multiply_kernel function.

    """

    let a: Array[Array[Float32]] = [[1.0, 2.0], [3.0, 4.0]]

    let b: Array[Array[Float32]] = [[5.0, 6.0], [7.0, 8.0]]

    let c: Array[Array[Float32]] = [[0.0, 0.0], [0.0, 0.0]]


    let start_time = now()

    matrix_multiply_kernel(a, b, c)

    let end_time = now()

    let elapsed_time = end_time - start_time
```

```
    print("Matrix Multiply Time:", elapsed_time)


fn main():

    """

    Demonstrates simple benchmarking.

    """

    benchmark_matrix_multiply()

}
```

Step-by-Step Explanation:

1. **Import** now **Function:** We import the now function from the `time` module.
2. **Define** `matrix_multiply_kernel` **Function:** (Same as in 4.1).
3. **Define** `benchmark_matrix_multiply` **Function:** This function benchmarks the `matrix_multiply_kernel` function.

4. **Create Test Matrices:** We create test matrices `a`, `b`, and `c`.

5. **Measure Start Time:** We record the start time using `now()`.

6. **Call Kernel Function:** We call the `matrix_multiply_kernel` function.

7. **Measure End Time:** We record the end time using `now()`.

8. **Calculate Elapsed Time:** We calculate the elapsed time.

9. **Print Elapsed Time:** We print the elapsed time.

10. **Main Function:** We call `benchmark_matrix_multiply`.

Practical Implementation: Profiling with Modular's Profiler (Conceptual)

Modular is actively developing profiling tools for Mojo. Here's a conceptual example to illustrate how we might profile our code.

- **Note:** Modular's profiling tools are subject to change. Consult the latest Mojo documentation for accurate and up-to-date implementation.

Code snippet

```
# Conceptual Example(subject to change)

# from profiling import profile_start, profile_stop


# fn matrix_multiply_kernel(a: Array[Array[Float32]], b:
Array[Array[Float32]], c: Array[Array[Float32]]):

#    # ... (matrix multiplication code) ...


# fn main():

#    profile_start("matrix_multiply")

#    matrix_multiply_kernel(a, b, c)

#    profile_stop("matrix_multiply")
```

Personal Insight:

When I started benchmarking and profiling my code, it was like shining a light into the dark corners of my program. I was able to identify bottlenecks that I never would have noticed otherwise. Also, be sure to benchmark on the same hardware as your target deployment. Hardware differences can have a big impact on performance.

Key Concepts to Remember:

- **Benchmarking:** Measuring performance under controlled conditions.
- **Profiling:** Identifying performance bottlenecks.
- **Performance Analysis:** Interpreting benchmarking and profiling results.

Chapter 5: Deployment and Scaling LLM Applications

We've done the hard work: optimizing our models and crafting custom kernels. Now, it's time to get these LLMs out of our development environments and into the hands of users. This chapter is all about deployment and scaling – turning our Mojo creations into robust, production-ready applications.

5.1 Strategies for Deploying Mojo-Powered LLM Applications

We've optimized our LLM code with Mojo, and now it's time to bring it to the real world. Deployment is a critical step, and choosing the right strategy can significantly impact performance and scalability.

Understanding Deployment Strategies

Deploying LLMs involves making them accessible to users and applications. The key strategies include:

- **Serverless Deployment:** Deploying LLMs as serverless functions, ideal for event-driven applications and cost-effectiveness.
- **Containerization:** Packaging LLMs into containers for consistent environments and easy deployment.
- **Dedicated Servers:** Deploying LLMs on dedicated servers or virtual machines for high-performance applications.
- **API Endpoints:** Exposing LLMs as API endpoints for seamless integration with other applications.

Practical Implementation: Deploying as a Simple API Endpoint (Conceptual)

Let's illustrate how we might deploy a Mojo-powered LLM as a basic API endpoint using Python and a framework like Flask.

- **Note:** This example uses Python to create the API wrapper. The Mojo inference code will be called from python.

Python

Python (using Flask)

```python
from flask import Flask, request, jsonify

import subprocess

import json


app = Flask(__name__)


@app.route('/infer', methods=['POST'])

def infer():

    try:

        data = request.get_json()

        input_data = json.dumps(data['input']) #Convert
python list to json string.


        # Call Mojo inference function

        result = subprocess.run(['mojo', 'inference.mojo',
input_data], capture_output=True, text=True)
```

```python
        if result.returncode != 0:

            return jsonify({'error': result.stderr}), 500


        output = json.loads(result.stdout) #convert json
string back to python list.


        return jsonify({'result': output})


    except Exception as e:

        return jsonify({'error': str(e)}), 500


if __name__ == '__main__':

    app.run(debug=True)
```

Step-by-Step Explanation:

1. **Import Libraries:** We import the necessary Flask
   and subprocess libraries.

2. **Create Flask App:** We create a Flask web application.

3. **Define** `/infer` **Route:** We define a route that handles POST requests for inference.

4. **Get Input Data:** We get the input data from the JSON request.

5. **Call Mojo Inference:** We use `subprocess.run` to execute the Mojo inference script (`inference.mojo`) with the input data as an argument.

6. **Handle Errors:** We check the return code of the Mojo script and return an error if it fails.

7. **Return Result:** We return the result of the Mojo inference as a JSON response.

8. **Run Flask App:** We run the Flask application.

Mojo Inference Script (inference.mojo Conceptual):

Code snippet

```
from python import Python

from json import JSONDecoder, JSONEncoder

from io import File
```

```
from sys import argv


fn run_inference(input_data: Array[Float32]) ->
Array[Float32]:

    # Replace with your actual Mojo inference logic

    var output_data: Array[Float32] = []

    for value in input_data:

        output_data.push(value * 2.0)

    return output_data


fn main():

    if argv.size() > 1:

        let json_input = argv[1]

        let decoder = JSONDecoder()

        let input_list = decoder.decode(json_input)

        var input_array: Array[Float32] = []
```

```
    for item in input_list:

        input_array.push(item.to_float32())


    let result = run_inference(input_array)


    let encoder = JSONEncoder()

    print(encoder.encode(result))

else:

    print("Error: No input data provided.")
```

Practical Implementation: Containerization with Docker (Conceptual)

Containerization with Docker provides a consistent environment for deploying LLMs.

1. **Create Dockerfile:**

Dockerfile

```
FROM python:3.9-slim-buster

WORKDIR /app

COPY requirements.txt .

RUN pip install -r requirements.txt

COPY . .

CMD ["python", "app.py"]
```

2. **Build Docker Image:**

Bash

```
docker build -t llm-api .
```

3. **Run Docker Container:**

Bash

```
docker run -p 5000:5000 llm-api
```

Personal Insight:

When I first deployed LLM applications, I was amazed by the simplicity of containerization. Docker made it incredibly easy to create consistent environments and deploy my models across different platforms. Also, I found that using serverless functions for event based LLM inference was very cost effective.

Key Concepts to Remember:

- **API Endpoints:** Exposing LLMs as web services.
- **Containerization:** Packaging LLMs into Docker containers.
- **Serverless:** Deploying LLMs as functions.
- **Scalability:** Designing deployment for high performance and high volume.

By choosing the right deployment strategy, you can make your Mojo-powered LLM applications accessible and scalable.

5.2 Scaling LLM Applications for Production Environments

We've deployed our Mojo-powered LLM application. Now, let's ensure it can handle the demands of a production environment. Scaling is crucial for maintaining performance and availability as traffic increases.

Understanding Scaling Strategies

Scaling LLM applications involves:

- **Horizontal Scaling:** Adding more servers or containers to distribute the workload.
- **Load Balancing:** Distributing incoming requests evenly across servers.
- **Auto-Scaling:** Automatically adjusting the number of servers based on traffic patterns.
- **Caching:** Storing frequently used results to reduce the load on the LLM.

Practical Implementation: Horizontal Scaling with Kubernetes (Conceptual)

Kubernetes is a powerful tool for orchestrating containerized applications, making horizontal scaling relatively straightforward.

1. **Create Deployment YAML:**

YAML

```
# deployment.yaml

apiVersion: apps/v1

kind: Deployment

metadata:

  name: llm-deployment

spec:

  replicas: 3 # Start with 3 replicas

  selector:

    matchLabels:

      app: llm-api
```

```yaml
  template:

    metadata:

      labels:

        app: llm-api

    spec:

      containers:

        - name: llm-container

          image: llm-api:latest # your docker image

          ports:

            - containerPort: 5000
```

2. **Apply Deployment:**

Bash

```bash
kubectl apply -f deployment.yaml
```

3. Scale Deployment:

Bash

```
kubectl scale deployment llm-deployment --replicas=5 #
Scale to 5 replicas
```

4. Auto-Scaling (Horizontal Pod Autoscaler):

YAML

```yaml
# hpa.yaml

apiVersion: autoscaling/v2

kind: HorizontalPodAutoscaler

metadata:

  name: llm-hpa

spec:

  scaleTargetRef:

    apiVersion: apps/v1

    kind: Deployment
```

```
  name: llm-deployment

minReplicas: 3

maxReplicas: 10

targetCPUUtilizationPercentage: 80
```

Bash

```
kubectl apply -f hpa.yaml
```

Step-by-Step Explanation:

1. **Deployment YAML:** The deployment YAML file defines the desired state of the application, including the number of replicas (instances) and the container image.
2. **Apply Deployment:** The `kubectl apply` command creates the deployment in the Kubernetes cluster.
3. **Scale Deployment:** The `kubectl scale` command manually adjusts the number of replicas.

4. **HPA YAML:** The HPA YAML file defines the auto-scaling policy, including the minimum and maximum number of replicas and the target CPU utilization.

5. **Apply HPA:** The `kubectl apply` command creates the Horizontal Pod Autoscaler in the Kubernetes cluster.

Practical Implementation: Load Balancing with Nginx (Conceptual)

Nginx can act as a load balancer, distributing traffic across multiple LLM instances.

1. **Nginx Configuration:**

Nginx

```
# nginx.conf

upstream llm_servers {

    server llm-server-1:5000;

    server llm-server-2:5000;

    server llm-server-3:5000;
```

```
}


server {

    listen 80;


    location /infer {

        proxy_pass http://llm_servers;

    }

}
```

2. **Run Nginx:**

Bash

```
docker run -p 80:80 -v
$(pwd)/nginx.conf:/etc/nginx/nginx.conf nginx
```

Step-by-Step Explanation:

1. **Upstream Servers:** The `upstream` block defines
   the list of LLM servers.

2. **Server Block:** The `server` block defines the Nginx server configuration.
3. **Proxy Pass:** The `proxy_pass` directive forwards requests to the upstream LLM servers.
4. **Run Nginx:** The `docker run` command starts the Nginx container.

Practical Implementation: Caching with Redis (Conceptual)

Redis can be used to cache frequently used LLM results.

1. **Redis Setup:**
   ○ Setup a redis server.
2. **Modify Python API:**

Python

```
# python flask example.

import redis

# ... other imports ...


redis_client = redis.Redis(host='redis', port=6379)
```

```python
@app.route('/infer', methods=['POST'])

def infer():

    # ...

    cache_key = json.dumps(data['input'])

    cached_result = redis_client.get(cache_key)

    if cached_result:

        return jsonify({'result': json.loads(cached_result)}),
200


    # ... Mojo inference ...

    redis_client.set(cache_key, json.dumps(output))


    return jsonify({'result': output})
```

Personal Insight:

When I started scaling LLM applications, I quickly realized the importance of automation. Kubernetes and load balancing tools like Nginx made it much easier to manage large deployments. Also, caching common results drastically reduced the load on the LLM servers.

Key Concepts to Remember:

- **Horizontal Scaling:** Adding more servers.
- **Load Balancing:** Distributing traffic.
- **Auto-Scaling:** Automatically adjusting resources.
- **Caching:** Storing frequently used results.

By implementing these scaling strategies, you can ensure your Mojo-powered LLM applications can handle the demands of production environments.

5.3 Cloud and Edge Deployment Considerations

We've covered general deployment strategies. Now, let's explore the specific considerations for cloud and edge deployments. These environments present unique challenges and opportunities for Mojo-powered LLM applications.

Understanding Cloud and Edge Deployment

- **Cloud Deployment:** Deploying LLMs on cloud platforms (AWS, Google Cloud, Azure) offers scalability, flexibility, and a wide range of services.
- **Edge Deployment:** Deploying LLMs on edge devices (smartphones, IoT devices, edge servers) reduces latency, improves privacy, and enables offline functionality.

Practical Implementation: Cloud Deployment with AWS Lambda (Conceptual)

AWS Lambda allows us to deploy LLMs as serverless functions.

1. **Package Mojo and Dependencies:**
   - Create a zip file containing your Mojo inference code and any necessary dependencies.
   - This might involve compiling your Mojo code to a native executable that can be called by AWS Lambda.

2. **Create Lambda Function:**
   - In the AWS Lambda console, create a new function.
   - Choose a runtime that can execute your compiled Mojo binary (e.g., a custom runtime).
3. **Upload Deployment Package:**
   - Upload the zip file containing your Mojo code and dependencies.
4. **Configure Lambda Handler:**
   - Set the Lambda handler to the entry point of your Mojo executable.
5. **Invoke Lambda Function:**
   - Use the AWS Lambda API or console to invoke the function with input data.

Conceptual Python Lambda Handler:

Python

lambda_handler.py

```python
import subprocess

import json


def lambda_handler(event, context):

    try:

        input_data = json.dumps(event['input'])

        result = subprocess.run(['./mojo_inference',
input_data], capture_output=True, text=True)
#mojo_inference is the compiled mojo binary.


        if result.returncode != 0:

            return {

                'statusCode': 500,

                'body': json.dumps({'error': result.stderr})

            }
```

```python
        output = json.loads(result.stdout)

        return {
            'statusCode': 200,
            'body': json.dumps({'result': output})
        }

    except Exception as e:
        return {
            'statusCode': 500,
            'body': json.dumps({'error': str(e)})
        }
```

Practical Implementation: Edge Deployment Considerations (Conceptual)

Edge deployments require careful consideration of resource constraints and latency requirements.

1. **Resource Optimization:**

- Compile Mojo code for the target edge device's architecture.
- Use Mojo's memory management features to minimize memory footprint.
- Optimize kernels for the edge device's CPU or GPU.

2. **Latency Reduction:**
   - Minimize network communication by performing inference locally.
   - Use Mojo's low-latency features to reduce inference time.

3. **Offline Functionality:**
   - Store model weights and data locally for offline inference.
   - Use Mojo's efficient data loading to minimize loading times.

4. **Security:**
   - Encrypt model weights and data to protect against unauthorized access.
   - Implement secure communication protocols for data transfer.

Personal Insight:

When I started exploring cloud and edge deployments, I was amazed by the flexibility and power of these environments. Cloud platforms offered incredible scalability, while edge devices enabled real-time, localized inference. When deploying to edge devices, the small runtime of Mojo, and its ability to create small binaries, greatly simplified the deployment process.

Key Concepts to Remember:

- **Cloud Deployment:** Scalability, flexibility, and services.
- **Edge Deployment:** Low latency, privacy, and offline functionality.
- **Resource Optimization:** Minimizing memory and CPU usage.
- **Latency Reduction:** Minimizing network communication and inference time.
- **Security:** Protecting model weights and data.

By understanding the considerations for cloud and edge deployments, you can effectively deploy your Mojo-powered LLM applications in these environments.

Chapter 6: Advanced Mojo Techniques and Best Practices

We've covered the fundamentals and dived into optimization. Now, let's talk about the finesse—the advanced techniques and best practices that separate a good Mojo developer from a great one, especially when tackling large-scale LLM projects.

6.1 Advanced Mojo Features for Complex LLM Projects

We've covered the fundamentals of Mojo and its application to LLM development. Now, let's explore some advanced features that become essential when tackling complex LLM projects. These features enable us to build highly efficient, scalable, and maintainable applications.

Understanding Advanced Mojo Features

These features include:

- **Metaprogramming:** Generating code at compile time for increased flexibility and performance.

- **Structured Concurrency:** Managing concurrent execution with fine-grained control and safety.
- **Advanced Memory Management:** Optimizing memory usage for large-scale LLM models.
- **Custom Data Types and Traits:** Creating specialized data structures and behaviors.

Practical Implementation: Metaprogramming with `constexpr`

`constexpr` allows us to perform computations at compile time, reducing runtime overhead.

Code snippet

from math import Float32

constexpr fn power(base: Float32, exponent: Int) -> Float32:

    """

    Computes the power of a number at compile time.

Args:

    base: The base number.

    exponent: The exponent.

Returns:

    The result of the power operation.

"""

```
if exponent == 0:

    return 1.0

elif exponent > 0:

    return base * power(base, exponent - 1)

else:

    return 1.0 / power(base, -exponent)


fn main():

    """
```

Demonstrates constexpr for compile-time computation.

"""

let result: Float32 = power(2.0, 10) # computed at compile time

print(result)

}

Step-by-Step Explanation:

1. **Define** `constexpr` **Function:** We define a function using the `constexpr` keyword, indicating that it should be evaluated at compile time.
2. **Compute Power:** We implement the power function using recursion.
3. **Use** `constexpr` **Function:** We call the `power` function with constant arguments. The result is computed at compile time and embedded in the generated code.

Practical Implementation: Structured Concurrency (Conceptual)

Mojo's structured concurrency is still evolving, but here's a conceptual example illustrating its potential.

- **Note:** Mojo's concurrency features are subject to change. Consult the latest Mojo documentation for accurate and up-to-date implementation.

Code snippet

```
# Conceptual Example(subject to change)

# from concurrent import TaskGroup


# fn process_data_chunk(chunk: Array[Float32]) ->
Array[Float32]:

#     # Process data chunk

#     # ...

#     return chunk
```

```
# fn process_data_parallel(data: Array[Array[Float32]]) ->
Array[Array[Float32]]:

#    var results: Array[Array[Float32]] = []

#    with TaskGroup() as group:

#        for chunk in data:

#            group.spawn(process_data_chunk, chunk)

#        for task in group:

#            results.push(task.result())

#    return results


# fn main():

#    let data: Array[Array[Float32]] = [[1.0, 2.0], [3.0, 4.0],
[5.0, 6.0]]

#    let results = process_data_parallel(data)

#    print(results)
```

Practical Implementation: Custom Data Types and Traits (Conceptual)

Mojo's ability to define custom data types and traits enables us to create specialized data structures and behaviors for LLM models.

- **Note:** Traits in mojo are still evolving. Consult the latest Mojo documentation.

Code snippet

```
# conceptual example.

# trait VectorOperations[T]:

#     fn add(self, other: T) -> T

#     fn multiply(self, scalar: Float32) -> T


# struct Vector[T]:

#     data: Array[T]
```

```
#     fn add[T: VectorOperations[T]](self, other: Vector[T])
-> Vector[T]:

#          # implement vector addition

#          # ...



#     fn multiply[T: VectorOperations[T]](self, scalar:
Float32) -> Vector[T]:

#          # implement scalar multiplication

#          # ...



# fn main():

#     # use the vector struct.

#     # ...
```

Personal Insight:

When I started working on complex LLM projects, I
realized the importance of code generation and
structured concurrency. Mojo's metaprogramming

capabilities allowed me to generate highly optimized code for specific LLM architectures, and its concurrency features provided fine-grained control over parallel execution. Also, creating custom data structures allowed for more readable and maintainable code.

Key Concepts to Remember:

- **Metaprogramming:** Generating code at compile time.
- **Structured Concurrency:** Managing concurrent execution safely.
- **Advanced Memory Management:** Optimizing memory usage.
- **Custom Data Types and Traits:** Creating specialized data structures.

6.2 Debugging and Profiling Mojo Code

Building complex LLM projects requires robust debugging and profiling tools. Mojo, being a relatively new language, is actively developing these features. However, we can explore the available tools and techniques to effectively diagnose issues and optimize performance.

Understanding Debugging and Profiling

- **Debugging:** Identifying and fixing errors in our code.

- **Profiling:** Analyzing the performance of our code to identify bottlenecks.

Practical Implementation: Basic Debugging with `print` Statements

While dedicated debuggers are evolving, we can use `print` statements to inspect variables and control flow.

Code snippet

- fn calculate_average(values: Array[Float32]) -> Float32:
- """
- Calculates the average of an array of Float32 values.
-
- Args:
- values: The input array.
-
- Returns:

- The average of the values.
- """
- let size = values.size()
- if size == 0:
-     print("Error: Empty array")
-     return 0.0
-
- var sum: Float32 = 0.0
- for value in values:
-     sum += value
-     print("Current value:", value, "Current sum:", sum) #debug print statement
-
- let average = sum / size
- print("Calculated average:", average) #debug print statement
- return average
-
- fn main():
-     """
-     Demonstrates basic debugging with print statements.
-     """

```
let data: Array[Float32] = [1.0, 2.0, 3.0, 4.0, 5.0]
let avg = calculate_average(data)
print("Average:", avg)

let empty_data: Array[Float32] = []
let empty_avg = calculate_average(empty_data)
print("Empty Average:", empty_avg)
}
```

Step-by-Step Explanation:

1. **Insert** `print` **Statements:** We insert `print` statements to display the values of variables and track the execution flow.
2. **Run the Code:** We run the code and observe the output.
3. **Analyze the Output:** We analyze the output to identify any unexpected values or behavior.
4. **Handle Errors:** We add conditional logic to handle potential errors, and print error statements.

Practical Implementation: Profiling with Time Measurement

We can measure the execution time of specific code sections to identify performance bottlenecks.

Code snippet

```
from time import now
from math import Float32
from algorithm import range

fn matrix_multiply_kernel(a: Array[Array[Float32]],
    b: Array[Array[Float32]], c: Array[Array[Float32]]):
    """
    Custom kernel for matrix multiplication.
    """
    let rows_a = a.size()
    let cols_a = a[0].size()
    let cols_b = b[0].size()

    for i in range(rows_a):
        for j in range(cols_b):
            var sum: Float32 = 0.0
            for k in range(cols_a):
```

```
        sum += a[i][k] * b[k][j]
      c[i][j] = sum

fn profile_matrix_multiply():
    """
    Profiles the matrix_multiply_kernel function.
    """
    let a: Array[Array[Float32]] = [[1.0, 2.0], [3.0, 4.0]]
    let b: Array[Array[Float32]] = [[5.0, 6.0], [7.0, 8.0]]
    let c: Array[Array[Float32]] = [[0.0, 0.0], [0.0, 0.0]]

    let start_time = now()
    matrix_multiply_kernel(a, b, c)
    let end_time = now()
    let elapsed_time = end_time - start_time

    print("Matrix Multiply Time:", elapsed_time)

fn main():
    """
```

- Demonstrates basic profiling with time measurement.
- """
- profile_matrix_multiply()
- }

Step-by-Step Explanation:

1. **Import** now **Function:** We import the now function from the time module.

2. **Define** matrix_multiply_kernel **Function:** (Same as in previous examples).

3. **Define** profile_matrix_multiply **Function:** This function profiles the matrix_multiply_kernel function.

4. **Measure Start Time:** We record the start time using now().

5. **Call Kernel Function:** We call the matrix_multiply_kernel function.

6. **Measure End Time:** We record the end time using now().

7. **Calculate Elapsed Time:** We calculate the elapsed time.

8. **Print Elapsed Time:** We print the elapsed time.
9. **Main Function:** We call
   `profile_matrix_multiply`.

Practical Implementation: Modular's Profiler (Conceptual)

Modular is actively developing profiling tools for Mojo. Here's a conceptual example to illustrate how we might profile our code.

- **Note:** Modular's profiling tools are subject to change. Consult the latest Mojo documentation for accurate and up-to-date implementation.

Code snippet

- # Conceptual Example(subject to change)
- # from profiling import profile_start, profile_stop
-
- # fn matrix_multiply_kernel(a: Array[Array[Float32]], b: Array[Array[Float32]], c: Array[Array[Float32]]):
- #   # ... (matrix multiplication code) ...
-

- # fn main():
- #   profile_start("matrix_multiply")
- #   matrix_multiply_kernel(a, b, c)
- #   profile_stop("matrix_multiply")

Personal Insight:

Debugging and profiling are essential skills for any developer. While Mojo's tooling is still evolving, the available techniques can help us effectively diagnose issues and optimize performance. I found that carefully placed print statements, and time measurement, were invaluable for initial debugging.

Key Concepts to Remember:

- **Debugging:** Identifying and fixing errors.
- **Profiling:** Analyzing performance.
- **Print Statements:** Inspecting variables and control flow.
- **Time Measurement:** Measuring execution time.
- **Modular Profiler:** (When available) A dedicated profiling tool.

6.3 Best Practices for Large-Scale LLM Development

Building large-scale LLM projects demands a structured approach. We need to focus on maintainability, scalability, and collaboration. Let's explore some best practices that can help us navigate these challenges.

Understanding Best Practices

These best practices include:

- **Modular Design:** Breaking down the project into reusable components.
- **Version Control:** Using Git for collaborative development and code management.
- **Automated Testing:** Writing unit and integration tests to ensure code quality.
- **Documentation:** Creating clear and comprehensive documentation.
- **Continuous Integration/Continuous Deployment (CI/CD):** Automating the build, test, and deployment process.

Practical Implementation: Modular Design with Mojo Modules

Mojo's module system allows us to organize our code into reusable components.

1. **Create a Module:** Create a separate Mojo file (e.g., `matrix_operations.mojo`).

Code snippet

```
# matrix_operations.mojo

from math import Float32

from algorithm import range


fn matrix_multiply(a: Array[Array[Float32]], b: Array[Array[Float32]], c: Array[Array[Float32]]):

    """

    Performs matrix multiplication.

    """

    let rows_a = a.size()
```

```
let cols_a = a[0].size()

let cols_b = b[0].size()


for i in range(rows_a):

    for j in range(cols_b):

        var sum: Float32 = 0.0

        for k in range(cols_a):

            sum += a[i][k] * b[k][j]

        c[i][j] = sum
```

2. **Import the Module:** Import the module into your main Mojo file.

Code snippet

```
# main.mojo

from matrix_operations import matrix_multiply

from math import Float32
```

```
fn main():

    let a: Array[Array[Float32]] = [[1.0, 2.0], [3.0, 4.0]]

    let b: Array[Array[Float32]] = [[5.0, 6.0], [7.0, 8.0]]

    let c: Array[Array[Float32]] = [[0.0, 0.0], [0.0, 0.0]]


    matrix_multiply(a, b, c)

    print(c)
```

Step-by-Step Explanation:

1. **Create Module File:** We create a separate Mojo file (`matrix_operations.mojo`) to define the matrix multiplication function.

2. **Import Module:** We use the `from ... import ...` syntax to import the `matrix_multiply` function into our main Mojo file (`main.mojo`).

3. **Use Module Function:** We call the imported function as usual.

Practical Implementation: Automated Testing (Conceptual)

Mojo's testing frameworks are evolving. Here's a conceptual example of how we might write unit tests.

- **Note:** Mojo's testing frameworks are subject to change. Consult the latest Mojo documentation.

Code snippet

```
# conceptual example

# from testing import assert_equal


# fn add(a: Int, b: Int) -> Int:

#     return a + b


# fn test_add():

#     assert_equal(add(1, 2), 3)

#     assert_equal(add(-1, 1), 0)

#     assert_equal(add(0, 0), 0)
```

```
# fn main():

#     test_add()

#     print("All tests passed!")
```

Practical Implementation: Documentation with Comments

Use clear, concise comments to explain your code.

Code snippet

```
fn calculate_average(values: Array[Float32]) -> Float32:

    """

    Calculates the average of an array of Float32 values.


    Args:

        values: The input array.
```

Returns:

    The average of the values.   .

"""

let size = values.size()

if size == 0:

    # Handle empty array case

    return 0.0

var sum: Float32 = 0.0

for value in values:

    # Accumulate the sum of values

    sum += value

let average = sum / size

return average

Personal Insight:

When I started working on large-scale projects, I realized the importance of modularity and automated testing. Breaking down the project into reusable components made it much easier to maintain and extend. Automated tests gave me confidence that my code was working correctly. Also, using a version control system like git, is non negotiable, for any team based project.

Key Concepts to Remember:

- **Modular Design:** Reusable components.
- **Version Control:** Git for collaboration.
- **Automated Testing:** Unit and integration tests.
- **Documentation:** Clear and comprehensive documentation.
- **CI/CD:** Automating the build, test, and deployment process.[4]

Chapter 7: The Future of LLMs and Mojo

We've explored the present, and now it's time to gaze into the crystal ball. Where are LLMs heading? How will Mojo shape the future of AI? Let's dive in.

7.1 Emerging Trends in LLM Technology

The landscape of Large Language Models (LLMs) is rapidly evolving. We're witnessing breakthroughs that are reshaping how we interact with AI. Let's delve into some of the most prominent emerging trends.

Understanding the Evolving LLM Landscape

The trends we're seeing are driven by a quest for:

- **Increased Efficiency:** Making LLMs faster and more resource-efficient.
- **Enhanced Reasoning:** Enabling LLMs to perform complex reasoning and planning.
- **Multimodal Capabilities:** Integrating LLMs with other modalities like images and audio.

- **Personalization and Customization:** Tailoring LLMs to specific users and tasks.
- **Responsible AI:** Addressing ethical concerns and ensuring fairness.

Key Emerging Trends

1. **Efficient Transformer Architectures:**
   - Traditional transformer models can be computationally expensive.[6] Researchers are exploring novel architectures that reduce this overhead.
   - **Trend:** Techniques like sparse attention, linear transformers, and hardware-aware model design are gaining traction.
   - **Commentary:** These advancements are crucial for deploying LLMs on resource-constrained devices and for scaling to even larger models.
2. **Retrieval-Augmented Generation (RAG):**
   - LLMs can sometimes hallucinate or provide outdated information. RAG addresses this by grounding LLM responses in external knowledge sources.

- **Trend:** RAG systems are becoming more sophisticated, incorporating techniques like knowledge graphs and dynamic retrieval.
- **Commentary:** RAG is a key enabler for building reliable and trustworthy LLM applications.

3. **Multimodal LLMs:**
   - LLMs are no longer limited to text. They're being integrated with images, audio, and video.
   - **Trend:** Models like multimodal transformers and vision-language models are demonstrating impressive capabilities in tasks like image captioning and visual question answering.
   - **Commentary:** Multimodal LLMs are opening up exciting new possibilities for human-computer interaction and content creation.

4. **Agentic LLMs:**
   - LLMs are starting to be used as agents, capable of planning and executing complex actions.

- **Trend:** Tools like function calling, and planning frameworks are enabling LLMs to interact with external tools and APIs.
- **Commentary:** This is a major step towards building more autonomous and intelligent AI systems.

5. **Federated Learning and On-Device LLMs:**
   - For privacy and latency reasons, there is a growing interest in running LLMs on edge devices.
   - **Trend:** Techniques like model distillation, quantization, and federated learning are enabling the deployment of smaller, more efficient LLMs on smartphones and other edge devices.
   - **Commentary:** This will enable more personalized and responsive LLM experiences, while also protecting user privacy.

6. **Ethical and Responsible LLMs:**
   - As LLMs become more powerful, it's crucial to address ethical concerns like bias, toxicity, and misinformation.

- Trend: Researchers are developing techniques for bias mitigation, toxicity detection, and explainable AI.
- Commentary: Responsible AI is not just a technical challenge, but also a societal one. We need to develop frameworks and guidelines for the ethical use of LLMs.

Personal Insight:

I've been particularly excited about the progress in multimodal LLMs. The ability to seamlessly integrate text, images, and other modalities is truly transformative. Also, the focus on responsible AI is very important. We need to be aware of the ethical implications of LLMs, and work to mitigate potential harms.

Key Takeaways:

- LLM technology is rapidly advancing, with a focus on efficiency, reasoning, and multimodality.
- RAG and agentic LLMs are enabling more reliable and autonomous AI systems.
- On-device LLMs are improving privacy and latency.

- Ethical considerations are paramount in the development and deployment of LLMs.

7.2 The Evolving Mojo Ecosystem and Community

Mojo is a relatively new language, but its ecosystem and community are rapidly growing. This growth is crucial for its adoption and long-term success, particularly in the demanding field of LLM development.

Understanding the Mojo Ecosystem and Community

A healthy ecosystem and community provide:

- **Libraries and Tools:** Essential resources for developers.
- **Documentation and Tutorials:** Learning materials for new users.
- **Community Support:** A place to ask questions and get help.
- **Collaboration and Contribution:** Opportunities to contribute to the language's development.

Key Aspects of the Evolving Mojo Ecosystem

1. **Modular's Development and Vision:**
   - Modular, the company behind Mojo, is actively developing the language and its tooling.
   - Their vision is to create a unified programming model for AI hardware, enabling high performance and portability.
   - **Commentary:** Modular's commitment to Mojo's development is a strong indicator of its potential. Keep an eye on the official Modular documentation and blog for updates.

2. **Library Development:**
   - As Mojo matures, we can expect to see the development of libraries for common LLM tasks.
   - **Trend:** Libraries dealing with linear algebra, tensor operations, and neural network building blocks are emerging.
   - **Commentary:** The development of robust and well-maintained libraries will greatly simplify LLM development in Mojo.

3. **Community Growth and Contributions:**
   - The Mojo community is growing rapidly, with developers sharing code, tutorials, and insights.
   - **Trend:** Online forums, GitHub repositories, and social media groups are becoming active hubs for Mojo developers.
   - **Commentary:** Active community participation is vital. Contribute your knowledge and code to help grow the ecosystem.
4. **Tooling and IDE Support:**
   - Integrated development environments (IDEs) and debugging tools are essential for efficient development.
   - **Trend:** Modular is working on providing robust tooling, and support for existing IDEs is increasing.
   - **Commentary:** As the tooling matures, the developer experience will improve significantly.

5. **Documentation and Learning Resources:**
   ○ Comprehensive documentation and tutorials are crucial for onboarding new Mojo developers.
   ○ **Trend:** Modular is actively improving the official documentation, and community-driven learning resources are emerging.
   ○ **Commentary:** Clear and accessible learning materials will accelerate Mojo's adoption.

Practical Considerations for Participating in the Mojo Community

- **Engage in Online Forums:** Participate in discussions and ask questions.
- **Contribute to GitHub Repositories:** Share your code and contribute to existing projects.
- **Write Tutorials and Blog Posts:** Share your knowledge and help others learn Mojo.
- **Report Bugs and Suggest Features:** Help improve Mojo by providing feedback.

Personal Insight:

I've been impressed by the enthusiasm and energy of the Mojo community. The developers are passionate about the language, and they're actively working to build a strong ecosystem. Also, the commitment of the Modular team is very encouraging. The pace of development is rapid.

Key Takeaways:

- The Mojo ecosystem and community are rapidly growing.
- Modular's development and vision are driving the language's progress.
- Community contributions and library development are vital for Mojo's success.
- Tooling and documentation are essential for a positive developer experience.

By actively participating in the Mojo community, we can contribute to its growth and help shape the future of LLM development.

7.3 Potential Future Applications of Mojo in AI

Mojo's unique blend of Python-like syntax and system-level performance opens up a world of possibilities for AI development.While we've focused on LLMs, Mojo's potential extends far beyond. Let's explore some potential future applications.

Understanding Mojo's AI Potential

Mojo's strengths make it well-suited for:

- **High-Performance AI Workloads:** Where speed and efficiency are critical.
- **Hardware-Aware AI:** Optimizing code for specific hardware architectures.
- **Complex AI Systems:** Building intricate AI applications that require fine-grained control.

Potential Future Applications

1. **Robotics and Autonomous Systems:**
   - ○ Robots and autonomous vehicles require real-time processing of sensor data and complex decision-making.
   - ○ **Potential:** Mojo's performance could enable the development of highly efficient perception and control algorithms. Hardware specific optimization is also very important in robotics.
   - ○ **Commentary:** The ability to write high-performance code that directly interacts with hardware could be a game-changer for robotics.

2. **Scientific Computing and Simulation:**
   - ○ AI is increasingly used in scientific simulations, such as climate modeling and drug discovery.
   - ○ **Potential:** Mojo's speed could significantly accelerate these simulations, enabling researchers to explore more complex models.
   - ○ **Commentary:** Mojo's ability to efficiently handle large datasets and complex

computations could make it a valuable tool for scientific computing.

3. **Computer Vision and Image Processing:**
   - Real-time image processing and computer vision applications, like augmented reality and video analytics, demand high performance.
   - **Potential:** Mojo's low-level control could enable the development of optimized image processing pipelines.
   - **Commentary:** The ability to leverage SIMD instructions and optimize memory access patterns could lead to significant performance gains in computer vision tasks.

4. **Game Development:**
   - Modern games use AI for tasks like character behavior, pathfinding, and procedural content generation.
   - **Potential:** Mojo's speed could enable the development of more complex and realistic AI in games.

- Commentary: Mojo's ability to create performant game engines, and game logic, is a very interesting avenue of exploration.

5. **Edge AI and IoT:**
    - Running AI models on edge devices is crucial for applications like smart homes, industrial automation, and healthcare.
    - **Potential:** Mojo's efficiency could enable the deployment of more complex AI models on resource-constrained devices.
    - **Commentary:** The ability to optimize code for specific edge hardware could be a key advantage.

6. **Custom Hardware Acceleration:**
    - As AI workloads become more specialized, there's a growing need for custom hardware accelerators (e.g., FPGAs, ASICs).
    - **Potential:** Mojo's low level control, could enable the creation of highly optimized software for these custom hardware platforms.
    - **Commentary:** Mojo has the ability to bridge the gap between high level programming,

and low level hardware, which is very important for custom hardware acceleration.

Personal Insight:

I'm particularly excited about Mojo's potential in robotics and edge AI. The ability to run complex AI models on resource-constrained devices could unlock a wide range of new applications. Also, the ability to write code that interacts directly with custom hardware, is a very interesting prospect.

Key Takeaways:

- Mojo's performance and low-level control make it suitable for a wide range of AI applications.
- Robotics, scientific computing, computer vision, game development, and edge AI are promising areas.
- Mojo's ability to work with custom hardware is a significant advantage.
- The future of Mojo in AI is bright, with potential to revolutionize high performance AI applications.

www.ingramcontent.com/pod-product-compliance
Lightning Source LLC
LaVergne TN
LVHW080116070326
832902LV00015B/2624